THE FIRST CHRISTMAS

Georgie Adams

Illustrated by Anna C. Leplar

BROADMAN
&HOLMAN
PUBLISHERS

Nashville, Tennessee

The story of Christmas is about a special birthday,
which happened in a country called Palestine,
a very long time ago.

It all began when an angel visited a young woman called Mary. The angel's name was Gabriel and he had come to give Mary a message from God.

Mary had heard all about angels but she had never *seen* one before. When Gabriel appeared, she was frightened.

"Don't be afraid," said Gabriel.

"God has chosen you to be the mother of His son.
He will be the most important baby ever born,
and you are to name him Jesus."

Soon afterwards, Mary married a carpenter called Joseph.
Another angel had told Joseph all about Mary's special baby,
and he promised to love Jesus, as if he were his own son.

Now at that time, the emperor of Rome was counting people, because everyone had to pay taxes - sums of money that helped to pay for the army and for building roads.

The emperor was working out how much money people had to pay him, by adding up all the people living in Palestine.

Everybody had to go back to the town where they were born to be counted. It was quite a business.

Mary and Joseph lived in Nazareth, but Joseph had been born in Bethlehem. So he and Mary were having to make the long journey to Bethlehem. It took them about a week.

Mary rode all the way on a donkey. By the time they got to Bethlehem Mary was very tired. Her baby was due at any moment!

"We must find somewhere to rest," said Joseph.
They went straight to an inn and pushed through a crowd
in the doorway. The innkeeper had to turn them away.
"Sorry," he said. "No room."
No room! Joseph was really worried.

They went from house to house looking for somewhere
to stay. But there were hundreds of visitors in Bethlehem,
and everywhere was full.

At last, when it was dark, they found a stable. The kind owner moved his animals into a stall, and gave Mary's donkey food and water. Mary made herself as comfortable as she could on a bed of straw. And that night, baby Jesus was born.

Mary gently wrapped her baby to keep him snug and warm. Joseph spread soft hay inside a manger. It made a good cradle. There, in the glow of an oil lamp, Mary and Joseph watched as the new-born baby slept.

In the hills around Bethlehem, shepherds were looking after their sheep. Although it was late at night, the shepherds were wide awake. Wild animals were always on the lookout for a stray lamb.

Everything was peaceful until the shepherds were startled by a brilliant light. They shielded their eyes from the glare, and were afraid.

Then a voice spoke out of the brightness. It was an angel.

"Don't be frightened," said the angel. "A king has been born in Bethlehem. The baby is God's son. Go and see him. You will find him in a stable, lying in a manger."

Well, the shepherds could hardly believe their ears.
They were amazed.

As soon as the angel had finished speaking, music filled
the air. All the angels in heaven were singing to God!

In a while the sound of their voices faded. The shepherds looked up at the stars, but the angels had gone.

"We must hurry to Bethlehem," said the shepherds, when they had recovered.

First they made sure their flocks were safe. Then they ran down the hillside and went to look for the new-born king.

The streets of Bethlehem were quiet as the shepherds searched for the stable. Suddenly they heard a noise. It was a baby crying! After that they found the stable easily.

"Come in," said Mary.

It was as if she were expecting them.

The shepherds went in and found Jesus in the manger - just as the angel had said.

Now there were three rich wise men, living in another country far away from Bethlehem. These men had spent many years studying the stars.

One night they saw a new star. It was brighter than any they had seen before. The wise men were sure it was a sign that a new king had been born.

So they loaded up their camels and followed the star. It led them over hills. Across deserts. Along rivers. That beautiful star guided them all the way to Bethlehem. It shone right over the stable where Jesus lay.

Mary and Joseph welcomed the three wise men in their fine clothes and jewels. But as soon as the wise men saw the baby Jesus, they knelt on the dusty floor and worshipped him.

The three wise men gave Jesus gifts of gold, frankincense and sweet-smelling myrrh - three special gifts fit for a new-born king.

And that's the story of the
very first Christmas long, long ago.